# What's the State Judicial Branch?
## Revised Edition

Nancy Harris

capstone

©2008, 2016 Heinemann Library
an imprint of Capstone Global Library, LLC.
Chicago, Illinois

To contact Capstone Global Library, please
call 800-747-4992, or visit our web site
www.capstonepub.com

Photo research by Tracy Cummins and Tracey Engel
Designed by Kimberly R. Miracle and Betsy Wernert

**Library of Congress Cataloging-in-Publication Data
is available on the Library of Congress website.**
  ISBN 978-1-4846-3691-6 (revised paperback)
  ISBN 978-1-4846-3496-7 (ebook)

**Photo Credits**
AP Photo: BEBETO MATTHEWS, 18, Chris Gardner, 22, Elizabeth Williams, 17, Jim McKNight, 20, The News & Observer/Juli Leonard, 21, Ted S. Warren, 23; Corbis: Tim Pannell, 15; iStockphoto: Arpad Benedek, 6, Deborah Cheramie, 10, 14, Rich Legg, 8; Map Resources: 4; Shutterstock: bikeriderlondon, Cover, 7, Fotoluminate LLC, 24, fstockfoto, 27, Joseph Sohm, 28, maxriesgo, 19, Pierre Desrosiers, 29, Stephen Coburn, 12, wavebreakmedia, 11; SuperStock: Flirt, 16; Thinkstock: Stockbyte, 9

Every effort has been made to contact copyright holders of any material reproduced in this book. Any omissions will be rectified in subsequent printings if notice is given to the publisher.

**Disclaimer**
All the Internet addresses (URLs) given in this book were valid at the time of going to press. However, due to the dynamic nature of the Internet, some addresses may have changed, or sites may have changed or ceased to exist since publication. While the author and publisher regret any inconvenience this may cause readers, no responsibility for any such changes can be accepted by either the author or the publisher.

Printed and bound in the USA.
072019      002412

# Contents

Some words are shown in bold, **like this**. You can find out what they mean by looking in the glossary.

# The State Judicial Branch

Each state has its own government. The state government leads the whole state. The state government is made up of people who are **elected** (chosen) to run the state.

> ★ State governments make decisions for people in their state.

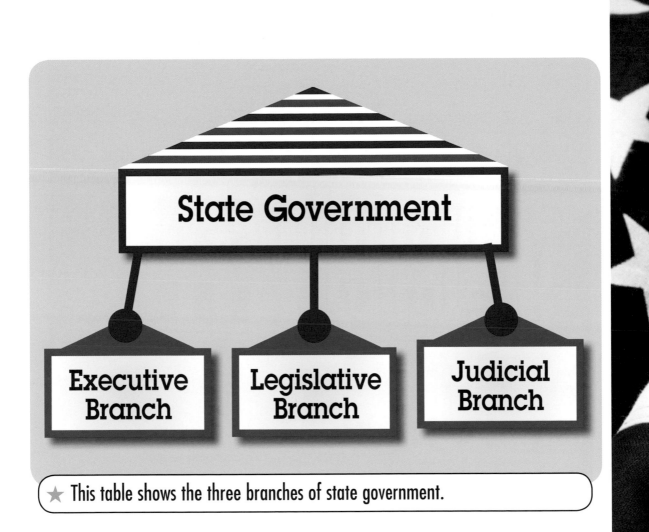

★ This table shows the three branches of state government.

The state government is made up of three branches (parts). Each branch has a special job. One branch is called the state judicial branch.

★ People in the state judicial branch work in courthouses.

People who work in the state judicial branch make sure that the **laws** (rules) of the state are understood. They decide if a state law has been broken.

# What Is a Judge?

★ Judges make decisions about laws.

**Judges** work in the state judicial branch. Judges know the laws. They decide if a state law has been broken.

★ Judges decide if a person has broken the law.

**Judges** are the leaders of **courts**. A court is a place people can go to settle an argument. They also go to court if they feel a **law** has been broken. People may go to court if they have been accused of breaking a law.

# What Is a Lawyer?

**Lawyers** also work in courts. They help people who go to court. They know the laws in their state. They talk to the judge for the person. These talks are called **cases**.

★★★ Lawyers use their understanding of the law to help people in court.

In a **case**, a **judge** hears two different arguments. For example, one **lawyer** tries to prove that a person has not broken a **law**. Another lawyer tries to prove that the person did break the law.

★ The judge acts like a referee in a case.

A case can last days or even months. The case usually ends with a decision about whether a law has been broken.

★ Judges must decide which argument they agree with.

# State Courts

★★★ Some people go to court without the help of a **lawyer**.

There are many **courts** in the state judicial branch. Each court has a specific job. For example, traffic courts hear **cases** that involve tickets for speeding. They also handle cases for other driving **violations** (crimes).

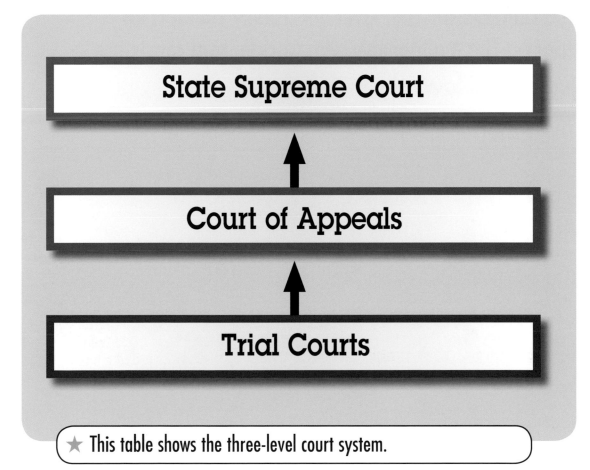

State Supreme Court

↑

Court of Appeals

↑

Trial Courts

★ This table shows the three-level court system.

Each state has its own **court system**. A court system has different levels of courts. In many states, there are three levels of courts. The lowest level is where people bring their case first.

# Trial Courts

The courts in the first level are usually called **trial courts**. The main people who work in trial courts are **judges** and **lawyers**.

★ Lawyers show documents to help prove their case.

★ Jury members must decide if a state **law** has been broken.

Some trial **cases** may be heard in front of a **jury**.
A jury is a group of **citizens** chosen to hear a court
case. Citizens are people who live in the state and
can vote.

If it is decided that a state **law** has been broken, a punishment is given. It is given to the person or people who have broken the law. The punishment depends on what kind of law has been broken. It could involve paying money or going to jail.

★ This person is reading the **jury's** decision on a case.

★
★
★ Cameras are not allowed in most U.S. courts. Instead, an artist makes drawings of what happens in a trial.

There are many types of **trial courts**. The trial court a person goes to depends on the type of **case** being heard. It also depends on the types of trial courts in the state.

★ **Judges** in family courts finalize adoptions.

For example, if the **case** involves family **law**, people go to a family **court**. Family courts hear cases about adopting a baby. They also hear cases to decide who can perform a marriage ceremony.

# State Court of Appeals

Sometimes the people involved in a case do not agree with the **trial court's** decision. They can **appeal** the decision and take the case to the second level in the state **court system**. They ask the court in the second level to make a new decision.

★ People must file papers to appeal their case.

In many states, the **court** in the second level is called the **Court of Appeals** or **Appellate Court**. This court can change the first court's decision.

★ A Court of Appeals may have several **judges**.

In a Court of Appeals, **lawyers** present the same **case** to judges. A Court of Appeals does not have a **jury**. Judges make a decision about the case.

Judge Elmore

★★★ Lawyers try to prove that the first decision in a case was wrong.

If the **judges** decide that a state **law** has been broken, they give a punishment. It can be the same punishment that the first **court** gave or a new punishment.

★ Judges listen to cases before making a decision.

★ Judges in the third level of courts hear the case again.

Sometimes the people who brought the **case** to the **Court of Appeals** do not agree with the court's decision. They can take the case to the court in the third level of the state **court system**.

# State Supreme Court

In most states, the **court** in the third level is called the **Supreme Court**. **Judges** in the state Supreme Court make a final decision on the **case**. If they decide a **law** has been broken, they give a punishment for the crime.

★ This is the state of Florida's Supreme Court building.

Some states have a two-level **court system**. In these states, the first level includes **trial courts**. The second-level court is usually called the Supreme Court. It has the same job as the Supreme Court in a three-level court system. It is the last court a case can be taken to in the state court system.

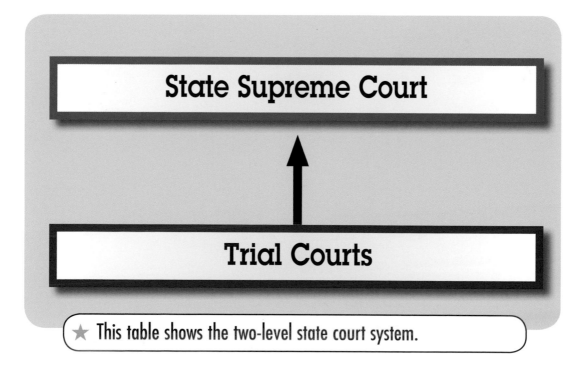

★ This table shows the two-level state court system.

# Other Courts in the United States

There are also **courts** outside the state judicial branch. They are called **federal courts**. Federal courts are part of the **federal government**. The federal government leads the whole country.

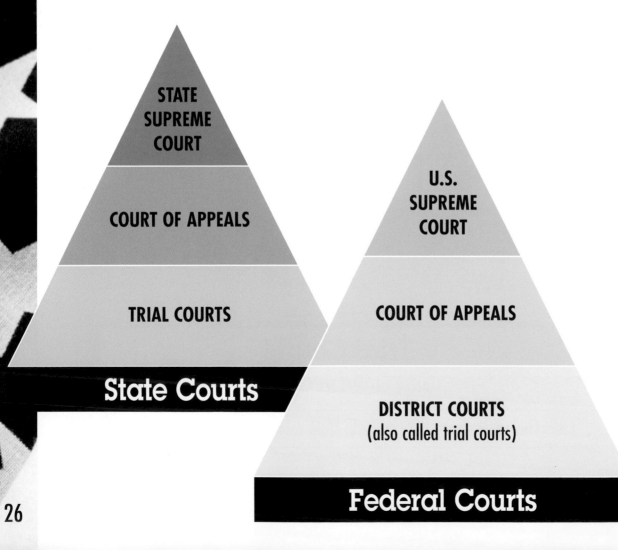

STATE SUPREME COURT

COURT OF APPEALS

TRIAL COURTS

State Courts

U.S. SUPREME COURT

COURT OF APPEALS

DISTRICT COURTS
(also called trial courts)

Federal Courts

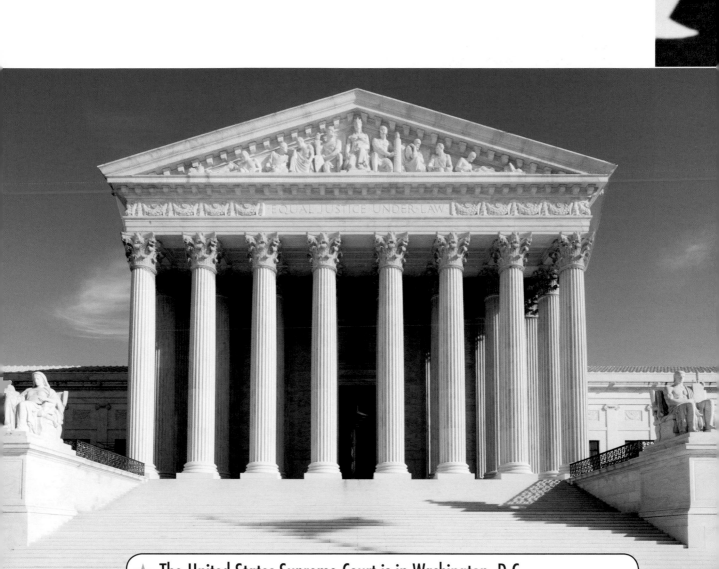

★ The United States Supreme Court is in Washington, D.C.

The United States Supreme Court is a federal court. It is the highest court in the country. It is the last court a **case** can be taken to in the federal goverment.

# How Do You Become a State Judge?

★ Citizens vote to choose their state and local judges.

Every state has different **laws** that say how a person can become a state **judge**. Some judges are chosen by the governor. Some judges are **elected** by **citizens**.

# Leading the State Justice System

The state judicial branch is an important part of the state government. This branch decides if state laws have been broken.

# Glossary

**appeal**  ask for another decision to be made on a case

**Appellate Court**  *see* Court of Appeals

**case**  public talk about a specific law or laws in a court. The talk is held to decide if a law has been broken.

**citizen**  person who is born in the United States. People who have moved to the United States from another country can become citizens by taking a test.

**court**  place where a case is heard

**Court of Appeals**  also called appeals court. Court where a judge looks over the decision made on a case by a lower court.

**court system**  group of courts in a state or in the federal government

**elect**  choose a leader by voting

**federal court**  court that is part of the United States federal government. The federal government runs the entire country.

**federal government**  government where a group of leaders run the entire country. In a federal government, the country is made up of many states.

**judge**  person who decides if a law has been broken

**jury**  group of citizens selected to hear a case in court

**law**  rule people must obey in a state or country

**lawyer**  person who knows the law. Lawyers help people who go to court. They try to get the judge to agree with the person's opinion.

**Supreme Court**  highest court in the state; the United States Supreme Court is the highest court in the country. It is in Washington, D.C.